# PATRICK FORSYTH

## the little book of
# NEGOTIATION

## HOW TO GET
### WHAT YOU WANT

Hero, 51 Gower Street, London, WC1E 6HJ
hero@hero-press.com | www.hero-press.com

Contents © Patrick Forsyth 2023
The right of the above author to be identified as the author of this work
has been asserted in accordance with the Copyright, Designs and Patents
Act 1988. British Library Cataloguing in Publication Data available.

Print ISBN 9781800313750
Ebook ISBN 9781800313767
Set in Times.

**Patrick Forsyth** has many years' experience working as a business consultant and trainer, specialising in communications and is also a writer. His writing goes further than the business area, including a humorous book (*Empty when half full*), three books of light-hearted travel writing (including *Beguiling Burma*) all set in South East Asia, and three novels (the most recent being *A Rather Curious Crime*). He has written previously about negotiation, and here explains the process and shows how to go about it in this new, unique, format.

## *NOTE*

*This book encapsulates the core principles and techniques of negotiating. It aims to inform and encourage good negotiation in the future, if you are interested in going further than the content possible in this format allows, note that the author, Patrick Forsyth, has also written the book "Negotiation" in the Legend Business Smart Skills series (under the name of Anthony Jacks).*

# PREFACE

Negotiation may seem a daunting word, but at its core it is only the interactive process of bargaining, something designed to secure a good deal. Whether it happens in sales (strictly after someone is persuaded to buy), for personal reasons (for example, negotiating a pay rise), or in political, corporate or international situations, the way it works is always similar.

It is to a degree a complex process, though the range of different stages and techniques are all individually manageable. Negotiation is not an argument, almost certainly demands compromise and also has a ritual aspect to it; it has to be gone about in the right way if it is to be successful.

The results of a successful negotiation are many and varied: it can help make things happen, prompt collaboration, save or make money and a successful negotiator has a valuable skill to use and deploy in personal and work life.

An overall understanding of the two and fro process involved is the first step to making it work. So let's start by focussing on the fundamental principles. Nothing sums it up better than the following (posted on the internet).

If you want a guinea pig,
first you ask for a pony

ANNABEL (Aged 6)

# FIRST, THE FUNDAMENTALS...

Negotiation is the process of identifying, debating, arranging and agreeing the, sometimes many, different *terms and conditions* of an agreement

Persuasion secures agreement. Negotiation only becomes relevant *after* someone has been persuaded (in principle) to take a course of action and acts to complete the process

The different elements (terms) to be agreed, large and small, tangible and intangible (called *variables*) are *traded* to create a balanced arrangement acceptable to both parties. It's an *active* process needing a well deployed approach

You don't get what you deserve,
you get what you negotiate

ANON

While it is necessarily an *adversarial* process with both parties wanting and striving to achieve the best deal for themselves, to be agreed any arrangement must satisfy both sides in what is referred to as a *win-win* outcome

When a man tells me he is going to put all his
cards on the table,
I always look up his sleeve

LORD HORE-BELISHA

Realistically neither party will win everything, but by trading variables (in whole or part) on an "if I do this... will you do that?" basis and always appearing to be driving a hard bargain, progress can be made and a point of balance found.

Identifying and *organising* the variables is a necessity. Consider both what they are (they may be numerous, make a list) and what their relative importance is. You can then use them in different ways as negotiations progress

It helps to imagine an old fashioned weighing machine, each side piled with items (variables) of different sizes and weights. To obtain agreement the balance must be (largely) evenly balanced. Changing the size and shape of each item corresponds to discussing and agreeing terms

Avoid just saying "no" to suggestions, say *what if...* and suggest alternative ways forward

The most common way people give up their power,
is by thinking they don't have any

ALICE WALKER

What gives you the power to influence events? *Reward:* offering something the other party wants; *Threat:* appearing to withhold something they want; *Factual evidence* proving your case; *Bogeys:* distractions that give you an edge

One more thing gives you power. *Confidence*: convincingly displayed (however much you feel it) it strengthens your credibility and your case

If you think you can, you can and if you think you can't, you're right

MARY KAY ASH

There are four overall rules. <u>First,</u> *Aim High.* Aim for the very best deal. You can always trade down, it is difficult to trade up.

To achieve the best outcome: *categorise the variables* -
consider what you *must* obtain, what you *ideally* should
obtain and what you can *trade*

Aiming high means that what you ask for first – the so-called *initial stance* – must be confidently bullish (because any compromise is going to be less)

While you aim high, you must also have a bottom line (which might be several potential mixes of different things). You _must_ _be prepared to walk away_ (because no deal may really be better than a bad one!)

Everything, and especially your willingness to walk away, must be expressed in a manner that prompts *belief*. Anything less weakens your position

<u>Second rule</u>: *discover or (intelligently) infer what the other party wants* – get their "shopping list". The more you know about them the better you will do

When I am getting ready to reason with a man, I spend one third of my time thinking about myself and what I am going to say; and two thirds thinking about him and what he is going to say

ABRAHAM LINCOLN

Knowing the other party may involve research, questioning or, most often, both. Active questioning, using *open* questions to gain information is a key part of negotiation

Beware of misjudging people you know, perhaps know well, they may act surprisingly differently wearing their negotiating hat

If you have to boil down your negotiating attitude to two things, you can do a lot worse than *question everything* and *think big*

MARK McCORMACK

<u>Third rule:</u> keep all the variables in mind all the time. Do not underestimate the complexities of negotiating, it is the interrelationship between the variables that demands flexibility and makes the process work

Fourth rule: *Keep searching for further variables,* be flexible (good negotiators are quick on their feet). Remember that (practically) everything can be made to be negotiable

It's a crunch moment when you are in negotiation. You suddenly see an opening in the hedge and dive through it even if you get scratched

LEN MURRAY

Trading involves discussion: sometimes dividing a variable into parts, always describing what you want and what you are prepared to trade in ways designed to prompt agreement

Always trade a variable *reluctantly*. Never just *give it away*. Your response must *maximise* the perceived value of any variable you allow to go, making it easier to get more in return

Similarly *minimise* the value of variables offered to you belittling them and not conceding that you are being given something significant. Always suggest that the balance is weighted in their favour

He that speaks ill of the mare will buy her

BENJAMIN FRANKLIN

It is especially important to be clear with *figures*: quote something as being *about* 10.356 %, and that inappropriate "about" will label you as less than numerate and invite someone in for the kill

*Amortising* costs when dealing with finances is a good example of a useful minimising effect (£100 per month seeming less than £1200 for a year)

Money isn't everything:
usually it isn't even enough

WOODY ALLEN

Before anything else,
preparation is the key to success

ALEXANDER GRAHAM BELL

Preparation is important: *always* do it. Be clear where you want to get to. Think about the other party, the variables and how the meeting may go

Ideally you need to run the kind of meeting *you* want (to allow your direction of it to predominate) and yet which *they* find acceptable

The meeting you want will be one you are in charge of, and the trick is to exercise some control in a way that appears helpful and is not overt

When two men ride of a horse,
one must sit behind

WILLIAM SHAKESPEARE
("Much ado about nothing")

If you don't know where you're going,
you will probably end up somewhere else

DAVID P CAMPBELL

Key to preparation is having *trading variables* always clearly in mind: what you can *devalue*, what you can *give*, what you are likely to be *offered* and what you seek to *get*

Be honest about your numeracy. When financial matters are involved, it may be well worth doing a number of calculations as part of your preparation

The essence of mathematics is not to make simple things complicated,
but to make complicated things simple

S. GUDDER

Any seasoned deal maker will tell you that spontaneous negotiation's a bad strategy; the ad hoc approach will leave you ripped-off, busted, conned, stiffed, out-smarted and generally holding the shitty end of the stick

GLEN DUNCAN

Whatever else you are doing at any point during a negotiation, from preparation to follow up, it is worth asking yourself: *Am I paying enough attention to the people problem?*

ROGER FISHER, BRUCE PATTON
and WILLIAM URY

While you need clout, your manner must always be acceptable, projecting a mixture of presence and empathy making you seem professional and indicating you consider other's viewpoint

It pays to be well-organised, and to *be seen* to be well-organised. Neat papers, facts and figures ready and stated with confidence, in all projecting the aura of a force to be reckoned with

It is only shallow people
who do not judge by appearances

OSCAR WILDE

Visible professionalism is important. Your manner must suggest experience, expertise and indicate someone negotiating with confidence, yet in a calm, considered way and with an underlying strength

If you look like a doormat, then people will likely walk all over you.

ANON

Always be prepared. Be organised: *Ready, aim, fire* is always likely to be the best order in which to proceed

Too many cooks spoil the broth

PROVERB

When more people than yourself are involved, think about a working pattern: who will lead, who will do what and how you will achieve a smooth handover between different individuals

The ultimate form of preparation is *rehearsal*. When there is complexity, and a great deal hanging on the outcome, taking time and effort to run over matters in advance is well worthwhile and will help ensure a meeting goes well

# SECONDLY, CORE TECHNIQUES TO DIRECT A NEGOTIATION...

Your careful deployment of techniques during a negotiation must help you make a clear case, manage the complexities of the trading process and drive the meeting towards a satisfactory outcome

Negotiating is akin to conducting an orchestra, you need to keep many balls in the air at once, but each one is manageable

Successful orchestration is key, it may take practice, but *is* possible; some people can juggle with flaming torches and not burn holes in the carpet

**Use your plan:** having prepared, keep your plan in mind, aim to move through its stages smoothly and direct the conversation towards your specific objectives

**Keep on track**: two-way conversation is unpredictable. Negotiating is rather like sailing a yacht, wind and tide take you off the straight line course, but knowing where your destination (objective) is, and being flexible, helps you correct as you go

**Communicate clearly**: avoid any confusion (and *never* underestimate its likelihood). Misunderstandings (especially financial misunderstandings) can be a momentary hitch or derail your whole case

I know you think you understood what
you think I said, but I am not sure
you realise that what you heard is
not what I meant

Attributed to RICHARD NIXON

**Engage the brain before the mouth:** Even a single sentence may need some thought, witness the sign saying: *It is dangerous to cross this bridge when this notice is underwater.* Key statements on complex (perhaps financial) issues may need especial consideration

**Be precise:** Make your case *understandable, attractive* and *credible*. Make individual points *succinct*, *specific* and *accurate* (especially with numbers)

**Select the right style:** Match your style to the occasion, your purpose and the nature of the other party

**Be logical:** having a clear sequence in mind as you present your case usually works best, keeping you on track and assisting in ensuring understanding

One should not aim at being possible to understand,
but at being impossible to misunderstand

MARCUS FABIUS QUNTILLIAN

No one will agree with something about which they are unclear. Ensuring total clarity is an absolute necessity in complex negotiating

**Watch for hidden misunderstandings**. People may fear displaying the fact that they have not understood and fail to check with questions

**Avoid obvious clichés:** saying such things as*: trust me – I am being totally honest* or *I'm a reasonable person* contributes nothing and may, at worst, suggest desperation

**Prompt them to start**: do not launch in with too much information early on, work to get them talking and giving you as much information as possible

**Ask questions**: negotiation is a dialogue and not a monologue. You need information about the other party's intentions and, while they will aim to keep their cards close to their chest, you must find out as much as possible

Better ask questions twice than lose your way once

DANISH PROVERB

**Get them talking**: yes and no answers help little. Use *open questions* to get people talking: What? Why? When? How? Where? Who? Also use *probing* questions – *tell me more about…* to dig deeper. Information brings power to your negotiating

**Listen to what they say:** listening is an *active* process, especially given the complexities of negotiation. Listen carefully, make notes if necessary and never assume or allow yourself to hear what *you want to hear*

We have two ears and one mouth
so that we can listen twice as much as we speak

EPICTETUS

**Clarify:** never continue unless you are absolutely sure what the other party means. Never hesitate to ask questions to clarify

**Check you are understood:** regular checks during a long meeting – *have I made that clear?* – help prevent misunderstandings

With good communication there are no surprises

T BOONE PICKENS

**Be patient**: take your time, do not rush discussion and remember that delay is better than a poor outcome. The ritual nature of to and fro negotiations make this a key rule

Patience and the passage of time do more than strength and fury

JEAN de La FONTAINE

**Regard the other party as an equal**: mutual respect oils the wheels of a discussion and prevents inappropriately personal arguments taking over

**Do not underestimate:** *never, ever* underestimate your opponent and be constantly vigilant for hidden motives and traps. A velvet glove may disguise an iron fist

Throwing an eleven foot rope to someone drowning twenty feet from the riverbank is more than meeting them halfway

LENNY BRUCE

**Avoid early difficulty**: it helps to build up rapport and momentum and not to get bogged down on contentious points, which are maybe best addressed later once a positive feeling has been created

**Hide your feelings**: an element of bluff is involved: if your face says *this is a minor point* when you respond to something major this can help your position

**Avoid stalemate**: do not push so hard that heels are dug in and progress ceases. Remember too that there is a line beyond which you get not a better deal but a complete breakdown

When a man says he approves something in principle,
it means he hasn't the slightest intention of putting it
into practice

BISMARK

**Avoid confrontation**: do not get trapped in a corner, avoid arguments, *never* lose your temper, rather always keep calm and stand firm

**Use outbursts:** a (very) *occasional* controlled outburst – *that's ridiculous!* – can demonstrate your firmness, but must *not* be overused (or allow anger to show)

**Use silence:** take your time and don't react too quickly. Silence unsettles people, implies you are confident and that what you say next will be well considered

Silence is even better than asking questions... it is always a hard argument to counter. Your opponent will give away his thoughts, approach, opinions, strategy. Talk less, learn more. There is weight in silence

MICHAEL SHEA

**Summarise frequently:** summarise to show where matters have got to (and, not least, what has been decided so far), also to avoid losing your thread in many faceted discussions as you juggle the variables

**Take notes:** you must keep track and not dilute your case by failing to remember some detail (particularly figures) already covered. Making notes can also give you a (perhaps useful) moment to think

**Promote good feeling:** negotiation builds agreement *progressively*. It helps create the right atmosphere if you stress the worth of each aspect or stage as you move along

**Read between the lines:** watch for danger signs in what is said. Remember negotiation is an adversarial process and a phrase like – *That's fair to us both* may well mean *That's just what I want*

The fellow that agrees with everything
you say is either a fool,
or is getting ready to skin you

FRANK McKINNEY HUBBARD

**Maintain neutrality:** as much and for as long as possible. Negotiation is a balancing exercise and you need to keep the focus on arrangements and not return to whether there is a deal to be done

**Keep thinking:** give yourself time to think and use it, do not let your mouth get ahead of your brain, and ensure everything you say is well-considered

A negotiator should observe everything.
You must be part Sherlock Holmes, part Sigmund Freud

VICTOR KYAM

**Hold your fire:** do not make an offer, certainly not a final offer, until everything that needs negotiating is out on the table

**Don't get hung up on deadlines:** *all aspects* of timing – how long things take, when things happen and in what order – are variables. It is said that there has never been a deadline in history that was not negotiable

I love deadlines. I like the whooshing noise they make
as they fly by

DOUGLAS ADAMS

**Remember that constraints and variables are interchangeable:** when something is said to be fixed, it likely indicates an attempt to *avoid* negotiating it. Remember that almost anything described as fixed can be made negotiable

**Don't crow:** when things are going well do not let your pleasure in a particular agreement show and especially avoid any "gotcha" comments

# FINALLY, A FEW MORE OVERALL CONSIDERATIONS...

**Some final don'ts**: do not over react, become emotional, lose your temper or your patience, be provocative or insulting, and do not push too hard. Such things can destroy the smooth path of a negotiation and maybe jeopardise the outcome too

Once an agreement is reached that is clear, agreed and noted, stop and rule a line. You do not want someone saying: *You know I've been thinking...* and find things are back to square one

Terms and conditions often form a complex mix. There can be a need for a *contract* – something in writing to secure the deal (if you feel this is necessary introduce the thought early and gradually)

A verbal contract isn't worth the paper
it is written on

SAMUEL GOLDWYN

Make sure the conclusion is win-win, if the other party feels they have been taken to the cleaners they will not be pleased – and may be unlikely to want to deal with you again

Negotiation is a social skill. Use the techniques that can make it work, do it, note what happens so that you learn from experience and, if necessary, do it differently and maybe better the next time

Practice makes perfect

PROVERB

Never believe you can wing it, never rely on good luck. Luck is only to be relied on to explain the success of those you dislike

Negotiations can have a great deal hanging on them. Good outcomes can make or save you money, prompt desired action immediately or on an ongoing basis and enhance your reputation. Consider the reverse and give attention to making things work

*A final thought: sometimes the results can be extraordinary:*

The best we ever heard of was the one who sold two milking machines to a farmer who only had one cow. Then they helped finance the deal by taking the cow as a down payment on the two milking machines

HERBERT PROCHNOW

Lightning Source UK Ltd.
Milton Keynes UK
UKHW021137020223
416355UK00008B/49